Who Cares About the Middle East?

"In this Orwellian era of indifference that empowers oppressors, caring as illustrated by authors like Kimbrough is a rare and welcome boost to the oppressed natives."

—MAZIN QUMSIYEH
Professor, Bethlehem University, Occupied Palestine

"These poems are short and to the point, ideal for use in meditation, in church gatherings, in political debates, and for social activism. My hope is that these poems will encourage reflection about justice, touch human hearts to reexamine their convictions, and trigger a just response to this just cause: Palestine."

—MITRI RAHEB
President, Dar al-Kalima University,
College of Arts and Culture Bethlehem, Palestine

"Kimbrough, historian and biblical scholar, writes passionate, Middle East-focused poetry in the classical style. If you have ever felt exhausted by the vitriol that poisons so many conversations about Palestine-Israel, give yourself the gift of revisiting these vitally important, heart-wrenching issues through the lens of poetry. Grounded in faith, hope, and love, Kimbrough's poems brim with humanity, social conscience, and a deep yearning for a just and lasting peace. Here are street-level scenes from Gaza and the West Bank, soul-convicting questions rising from human pain, and the indefatigable hopes of an oppressed people. Kimbrough's poems, especially about the children caught in this tragedy, take us there, challenge us to reflect anew, and call forth from us a humane response to this searing, century-long crisis."

—J. MARK DAVIDSON
Executive Director, Voices for Justice in Palestine

Who Cares About the Middle East?

Poems for Reflection and Conviction

S T Kimbrough Jr.

Foreword by Mitri Raheb

RESOURCE *Publications* • Eugene, Oregon

WHO CARES ABOUT THE MIDDLE EAST?
Poems for Reflection and Conviction

Resource Publications
An Imprint of Wipf and Stock Publishers
199 W. 8th Ave., Suite 3
Eugene, OR 97401

www.wipfandstock.com

PAPERBACK ISBN: 978-1-6667-0460-0
HARDCOVER ISBN: 978-1-6667-0461-7
EBOOK ISBN: 978-1-6667-0462-4

AUGUST 19, 2021

This book is dedicated to Burhan, Marwan, and Rami Ghanayem, who witnessed the birth of many of these poems, for their long-standing friendship and understanding.

Contents

Foreword

WHO CARES ABOUT THE Middle East? People in the Middle East regularly ask themselves this question. Over the past 100 years, the Middle East has been through twenty-six wars, not because the inhabitants of the region are violent and uncivilized, but because the geopolitical location connects three continents and controls three of the key waterways of the world: the Strait of Hormuz, the Strait of Gibraltar, and the Strait of Tiran; because the region has rich natural resources with over fifty percent of the world's proven oil and natural gas reserves; and because it represents the heart of the Arab and Muslim world.

Diverse empires — Ottoman, French, British, American, and Russian — have fought to control and colonize the Middle East. Following WWI, the region was divided up to serve the interests of the European empires. Following WWII and the subsequent Cold War, the region was divided between East and West, and regional powers (Israel, Turkey, Iran, Saudi Arabia, and the Gulf states) that are currently waging proxy wars in Syria, Lebanon, Yemen, Libya, and beyond. At the heart of the Middle East is Palestine, now the subject of the last European settler colonial project represented by the State of Israel and one of the longest ongoing occupations in modern history. This occupation would not continue if it were not for the military, financial and yes, the theological support of the Western world. The people of the Middle East feel that Europe and the United States care about the State of Israel and those of Jewish faith, but not so much about the Palestinians who are Arab Muslims and Arab Christians. To a large extent, Palestinians feel abandoned by both the West and by many neighboring Arab countries.

Who does care about the Middle East? S T Kimbrough does. An Old Testament professor, for him the Middle East represents the cradle of the three monotheistic religions, and the geographic and cultural context of salvation history. He is very well versed in the history, archaeology, and biblical background of the Middle East, particularly Palestine. Professor Kimbrough is also well acquainted with the modern Middle East and all its complexities. He is not afraid to tackle the socio-economic and political realities. His powerful poems are rooted in a deep understanding and the courage to call things by their true name. He describes the ongoing Israeli occupation and colonization of Palestinian land and people as it is: apartheid. He is aware that this statement comes with a price tag. When President Carter published his book *Palestine: Peace not Apartheid*[1] in 2007, with the warning that Israel was rapidly approaching a situation of apartheid, he was attacked vehemently by the Israel lobby and by Christian Zionists. Earlier this year, the Israeli human rights organization B'Tselem released its position paper entitled: *This is Apartheid: A regime of Jewish Supremacy from the Jordan River to the Mediterranean Sea.* In summary the paper stated:

> The Israeli regime enacts in all the territory it controls (Israeli sovereign territory, East Jerusalem, the West Bank, and the Gaza Strip) an apartheid regime. One organizing principle lies at the base of a wide array of Israeli policies: advancing and perpetuating the supremacy of one group — Jews — over another — Palestinians.
>
> B'Tselem rejects the perception of Israel as a democracy (inside the Green Line) that simultaneously upholds a temporary military occupation (beyond it). B'Tselem reached the conclusion that the bar for defining the Israeli regime as an apartheid regime has been met after considering the accumulation of policies and laws that Israel devised to entrench its control over Palestinians.
>
> The key tool Israel uses to implement the principle of Jewish supremacy is engineering space geographically, demographically, and politically. Jews go about their

1. Jimmy Carter, *Palestine: Peace Not Apartheid.*

lives in a single, contiguous space where they enjoy full
rights and self-determination. In contrast, Palestinians
live in a space that is fragmented into several units, each
with a different set of rights — given or denied by Israel,
but always inferior to the rights accorded to Jews.[2]

Professor Kimbrough is well aware of these realities on the
ground but his focus is on the people. At a time when the people
of the Middle East are negatively stereotyped by media outlets,
Kimbrough looks beyond mere numbers and statistics to see the
human beings with names, faces, stories, and potential. He cares
that behind the geopolitical facts are real people who are suffer-
ing, who are denied equality, dignity, and humanity. Kimbrough is
especially concerned with the children of the region who continue
to pay the heaviest price and are denied a childhood. His concerns
are not new and were evident at the heart of his earlier collection
of poems: *Why Should a Child Be Born?*[3]

As an Old Testament scholar, Professor Kimbrough is
very much influenced by the Old Testament prophets. Like them,
he understands the larger political picture; like them, he writes in
a poetic language; like them, he sees and feels the injustice that is
crying to the heavens; and like them, he cares about those who
are marginalized and powerless. He is not fooled by those false
prophets who utter words of peace when in reality no peace exists.
The so-called peace process between Israelis and Palestinians has
lasted almost thirty years but has proved to be less peace and more
a process that facilitates ongoing colonization and deepening oc-
cupation. Like the prophets, Kimbrough is passionate about one
thing: justice. He knows that peace can only be the fruit of justice:
justice for the oppressed, freedom for the imprisoned, and dignity
for those crushed under a military regime.

Religion, any religion, can often side with power and be
used to spread hate rather than understanding. As a historian,
Kimbrough is aware that Christianity has often propagated the

2. https://www.btselem.org/publications/
fulltext/202101_this_is_apartheid

3. Kimbrough, *Why Should a Child Be Born?*

ideology of the ruling empire rather than remaining faithful to the teachings of the incarnated and crucified Lord. As a Christian, he believes that religion has the potential to be part of the solution, to speak truth to power, and to imagine a different reality where all are equal before the law because all are important in the eyes of God. No wonder that Kimbrough's last poem is infused with prophetic imagination and a vision of one state in which no one is trapped behind a wall, and where all are truly free regardless of race or religion.

Kimbrough is passionate about the Middle East and about Palestine because he cares. He wants to make a difference, to fight for justice, to bring about change. But how to achieve this when the world has become so numb and weary of *the hundred year war on Palestine*?[4] Kimbrough chooses to address the human conscious-ness. His weapon is the written word, simple but powerful poems. These poems are short and to the point, ideal for use in meditation, in church gatherings, in political debates, and for social activism. My hope is that these poems will encourage reflection about jus-tice, will touch human hearts to reexamine their convictions, and may trigger a just response to this just cause: Palestine.

Rev. Dr. Mitri Raheb
President, Dar al-Kalima University
College of Arts and Culture
Bethlehem — Palestine

4. Khalidi, *The Hundred Years War on Palestifne*.

Introduction

JUSTICE HAS TO DO with the quality in our lives of being just and reasonable, and peace should be the result of justice. In one part of the world in particular, namely Israel and Palestine, many aspects of justice have a daily effect on the lives of those living there. This small collection of poems relates specifically to the Israeli occupation of Palestinian land, which has lasted for decades in both the twentieth and twenty-first centuries and about which I have written before.[1] It is the long-lasting nature of the occupation, which keeps it front and center on the stage of world diplomacy and violence, that the Israeli government continues to expand settlements on Palestinian land leaving them less and less space to exist. Of course, the brutalities resulting from the occupation are drastic indeed.

There are difficult challenges, such as displaced persons, lack of neighborly love, antisemitism, and apartheid, which I have addressed in some of these poems. The poems make no claim at lasting solutions, other than the realization that all human beings deserve respect from one another and that human dignity is a universal principle upon which all society must be based. For some these are merely placid assertions. I have written about some very specific instances of violence and prejudice in the lives of Israelis and Palestinians and queried how one can move beyond them.

To those who are radicalized with hate for the other, there often seems to be little hope. But if human beings are truly human, they cannot give up hope. It is often children who help us to see beyond our prejudices and hopelessness. The poem "Love

---

1. See my volume, *Why Should a Child Be Born? Poems for Peace and Justice in the Middle East.* Eugene, OR: Wipf and Stock Resource Publications, 2018.

Your Neighbor" is not a mere Pollyanna view of how things might be in a dream world. It is about two neighbors, an Israeli boy and a Palestinian boy, who can help us to see that all is not hopeless. Their story reminds me of the stories I have heard of times before 1948 when Jews and Palestinians lived side by side and respected one another as neighbors. These stories set the stage of a historical precedent for a one-state solution where all people live with equal rights!

The poems here are divided in five sections.

(1) *Apartheid*. The reality is that as each day passes Jews and Palestinians living within the bounds of historic Palestine and other Israeli occupied territories are moving more quickly than many parts of the world imagine to a distinctively apartheid state with separate laws making Jews a privileged class and Palestinians a marginalized and poverty-stricken class.

(2) *Children*. Palestinian children are one of the most gravely denied parts of the population. The deaths of and injuries to Palestinian children at the hands of Israeli government authorities and settlers, rarely make international channels of communication, but they are a reality. One need only observe the tremendous gap between the educational opportunities for Jewish children and those offered Palestinian children. Yet, even for those Palestinians holding appropriate Israeli identity documents, this makes little difference.

(3) *Faith*. Regardless of the sincerity with which Jews and Palestinians live out the principles of Judaism, Islam, and Christianity, leaders of these faiths willingly speak of the Holy Land in some form or another, which embodies holy sites cherished by all of them. It is almost ludicrous to think that in a land of three great religions, Jewish, Christian, and Muslim no way can be found to solve differences, while they reverently offer prayers to the Divine. Earnest faith and adherence to an ethic of justice embedded in all three of these faiths might do more than one might think to lead toward peace, if it were indeed practiced.

(4) *Injustice*. Unquestionably there are Jewish and Palestinian injustices, but Jews are the ruling, occupying, and privileged power,

and the Palestinians are the weak, impoverished, and second-class citizens locked into an apartheid system. The poems in this section indeed highlight the injustices against the Palestinians as an oppressed people. They seek to let justice speak for itself, knowing that facts speak truth unless distorted.

(5) *Peace.* Things have not changed very much from the time of the prophet Jeremiah who declared, "They have dressed the wound of my people with very little care, saying, 'Peace, peace,' when there is no peace at all. They dress the wound of my people as though it were not serious. 'Peace, peace,' they say, when there is no peace. They offer superficial treatments for my people's mortal wound" (Jeremiah 6:14). The mortal wound of the people of the Holy Land has not changed. It has simply widened its scope to include division, displacement, and distrust. Hence, we ask: Who is really serious about a cry for peace?

These poems are not intended as problem solvers, as such. They are written to precipitate serious thinking about a part of our world whose various religions claim to know the meaning of justice, but they do not demonstrate this as a reality. Of course, these religions are not in themselves political powers, although often religious beliefs spill over into the political arena.

Perhaps the turn of a poetical phrase may help us think in ways we have not thought before. Perhaps this may help us revise our thinking, and teach us anew what it means, above all else, to be human beings treasuring dignity for all. *Thus, just reflection can lead to just conviction and just response.*

S T Kimbrough Jr.

Section 1

Apartheid

1. Apartheid is Alive and Well

(at a West Bank Checkpoint)

Guard: I need to have your ID card,
                   young woman, I need yours?
           Without them both of you are barred
                   from going with these tours.

Palestinian father: "They're friends of ours from overseas,
                   to visit holy sites.
           Our IDs are you going to seize?
                   But what about our rights?"

The guard held them three hours or more,
                   while our friends traveled on.
Then said, as if he kept a score,
                   "Now pass, the tours are gone."

Checkpoints, permits, dividing walls,
                   some live with them each day.
Required by laws that one appalls,
                   apartheid has its way.

Alas, there is detention too,
                   without a charge or trial.
If you the laws' restrictions knew,
                   how base they are, how vile!

Apartheid is alive and well
                   through legislative schemes
that make the West Bank living hell,
                   devoid of any dreams.

2. Full Humanity?

Can there be full humanity
    without equality for all,
when politics and vanity
    seek bigger guns, a taller wall?

Humiliate those you oppose,
    defame their religion and race.
Like Zionism, I suppose,
    and crave to leave others no space.

Systemic discrimination
    results in an apartheid state.
How tragic to build a nation
    by dispossessing land and hate.

No people have the right to claim
    more rights than those of another.
If done, they bring eternal shame
    on every sister and brother.

Palestinians, Jews of color
    the racists' prejudice must bear;
some are forced to live in squalor!
    Where is there justice? Justice? Where?

From Ethiopia once came Jews[1]
    to Israel seeking a new life,
but skin of ebony, dark hues
    brought Jews from Africa new strife.

"Justice! Justice! Justice! for all,"
    the lasting and enduring cry.
Without it a nation will fall.
    Without it a nation will die!

---

1. These were Ethiopian Jews (Falashas) who camped on King David Street in Jerusalem in the summer of 1963 with huge signs saying: "Israel Practices Apartheid." This was not recently. It was fifty-nine years ago. They had been settled under extremely dire conditions near the Dead Sea. They used Ge'ez as their liturgical language not Hebrew. They were not even officially recognized as Jews until 1975.

3. An Israeli Sham and Shame

In Israel there's a new law,
    "Nationality" by name.
It clearly states without a flaw
    its sole and single aim.
So, if your mother is a Jew,
    you're citizen first class
But Arab mothers, nothing new,
    it segregates *en masse*.

Inferior are all non-Jews
    according to this law.
And certainly, it is not news:
    this law they'll not withdraw.
So now racism is the law,
    apartheid wins the day!
A chance the Jews will this withdraw?
    "It's justice!" they will say.

4. Persona non Grata

Turks cry, "Persona non grata!"
    and immigrants expel!
But mothers, children cry, "What a
    grim path leads us to hell."

They drive us toward the state of Greece;
    the Greeks teargas us there.
The children's burning, tears increase
    where can we go, but where?

We are just humans, nothing more.
    Is it too much to ask?
Humanely treat us now! What for?
    It's a disgusting task?

On, on it goes, this game of chess
    with human, living pawns.
It matters not the pain nor stress,
    or if a "welcome" dawns.

Humane behavior's yet to come
    to immigrants who flee.
Who'll dare to give them a new home?
    Such friends as you and me?

5. One Race

What pity that our common sense
    betrays the common good,
if 'round our thoughts we build a fence
    and don't do as we should.
If we think we are always right
    and others must be wrong,
on humankind we are a blight:
    all to one race belong!

One race there is, the human race
    with cultures manifold,
with varied thoughts that one can trace,
    ideas often bold.
Respect, however, there must be
    for one another's life:
for thoughts and language, sanctity,
    without rank hate or strife.

For brothers, sisters all are we,
    the human race we are.
Our differences each one can see
    must not the other mar.
If others see in us a friend,
    someone who's filled with care,
our lives in friendship soon will blend:
    the human race's dare!

Section 2

Children of Palestine and the Middle East

6. Mossaad Ibrahim

The young boy Mossaad Ibrahim
        was only three-years old,
yet murdered by a racist's scheme,
        by hatred, uncontrolled.

How innocent a child at prayer
        with family beside,
no longer will their love he share;
        there in the mosque he died.

A white supremacist fired rounds
        of bullets at the crowd
with frightening, loud-cracking sounds;
        some died where they had bowed:

where they had bowed to offer prayer
        came hatred, that disease.
The murderer had little care
        that they knelt on their knees.

To slay the innocent at prayer,
        to take life from a child,
can folk of faith quickly ensnare
        till anger has them riled?

There has to be another way
        than hate with hate to fight,
than slaying those who us would slay,
        for hate's a human blight.

Let us remember Mossaad's name
        each boy and girl of three.
Condemn all hate, loudly acclaim:
        Love all; this is life's key!

7. Beauty for an Injured Boy

How can a boy of six years think
  of beauty in the world,
when all around, life's on the brink,
  of war bombs being hurled.
Hurled at his house, in Gaza's strip,
  which yesterday was bombed,
and now he limps with injured hip;
  his nerves cannot be calmed.

Shall he have time for nature's gifts,
  to see the joys of life?
Or will he only see the rifts
  that bring the world its strife?
How can we beauty to him show?
  a rainbow in the sky?
Or will he only suffering know
  and ask forever, Why?

War mongers, it is time to heed
  creation's desperate cry:
"Stop, look, and see the world in need
  of beauty's lasting sigh!"
The sigh, the cry, the lasting pause
  creation now would make:
to render beauty's lasting cause
  eternal for our sake.

Who'll show such beauty to this boy,
    who now just limps along?
How will he ever find the joy
    that gives his heart a song?
The world must show this child the art
    of beauty for his soul
or it will never do its part
    to make him once more whole.

8. An Orphan's and a Nation's Fate

In body, mind, and spirit stunned,
shattered beyond belief,
a stumbling, wandering pantomime,
a child, weaves to and fro,
along a lonely road,
no one to hold her hand.

Disheveled, shocked, her blank-
frail-staring mien
reveals a horrid tale:
by morning light her home was stormed
by soldiers armed with guns.
She heard her mother crying, plead
"Mercy, mercy, mercy, please!"

Her father, brothers quickly bound,
beneath a blanket she lay still,
unnoticed by the raiding force.
Just then, the leader spoke out loud:
"The government has come today
to take your property, your land
to which you have no rights.
You men will go to jail."

The mother too they forced to leave
her lifelong-family home.
Her daughter of nine years, alone,
by no one had been seen,
orphaned in minutes by the claim:
Her parents, family had no rights.
A rare occurrence, dare you think?
No, daily this transpires.

The overflow of orphans shows
how tragic is the case!
No nation worth existence
in apathy can turn away.
Ignore the plight of orphans,
and as Rome burned and fell,
this fate will you befall!

9. Learning from Children

Some children born in Palestine
    in Syria, Yemen, and Iraq,
have lost their legs caused by a mine,
    on which they stepped, a deadly shock.
One happy, playful afternoon
    their friends were laughing all around.
But one false step and all were strewn
    across the blistering, writhing ground.

A mine burst where they liked to play;
    a deadly silence swiftly reigned
across the scene where they then lay.
    Some groaned, while life from others drained.
What more horrific can there be
    than children's lives destroyed by war?
Some may survive, but cannot see
    what purpose they are living for.

Their legs are gone, they cannot walk.
    they cannot run, and laugh, and play.
From shock and pain, they cannot talk,
    and yet, there dawn's another day.
Are there no human beings left,
    who'll stop this dastardly display
of hate and violence, greed, and theft
    of children's lives? Is there no way?

I know one hears of many a view,
 but children playing on that day
were Muslim, Christian, yes, and Jew.
 My! What a truth did they display!
We live, we play, we die as one;
 we hope for strength to struggle on.
Our task on earth cannot be done
 till all the barriers are gone.

10. Mourning One's Sons

My sons threw rocks, then I heard shots;
        they had no chance against the guns.
Aged eight and ten they'd made no plots,
        still soldiers killed my only sons.

From birth, they've lived in Gaza's strip;
        they've known no other place called home.
They never made a single trip
        to see the Holy City's dome.

When you grow up and have no rights
        to travel in your own home land,
when you've seen bombings and street fights,
        and no school regularly planned,

you grow up knowing you're deprived;
        you grow up seeing soldiers, guns.
You're thankful when you have survived,
        but on this day, they killed my sons.

11. Orphans of War

Remembering the Orphans of Syria and Yemen

How dastardly tyrants of war
    think nothing of to bomb
a family of members four
    and execute the mom.

The father of two little boys
    survived for just an hour.
His screams were heard above the noise,
    his injuries were dour.

Amid the rubble his two sons
    sit stunned but cannot cry,
for trauma through their bodies runs:
    they've seen their parents die!

In seconds orphans can be made
    by thoughtless, evil acts
and worse, the cost of death is paid
    by children; these are facts!

They pay, for orphans have no one
    to give them daily care;
and food for just one meal, there's none,
    nowhere to sleep, nowhere!

12. The Origin of Hate

An infant Muslim, Christian, Jew
    does not know how to hate.
For every child that's born it's true:
    hate birth does not create.

Adults are those who build the walls
    that hatred children teach.
These walls are worst of all pitfalls,
    for they create hate speech:

"Immured from others not like you
    "you must forever be.
"Don't think like them, do what they do;
    "with them never agree!"

If infants in their childhood hear
    a parent say such things,
then love and peace will disappear,
    the truths from which hope springs.

Tear down the wall 'round Bethlehem,
    the wall 'round Hebron too!
As infants grow they won't see them,
    as if they never knew.

Remove the symbols of all hate;
    remove the words that wound.
Then we'll with confidence await
    a world to peace attuned.

13. Yaser Abu al-Naja[1]—Who?

Yaser Abu al-Naja—Who?
    a boy of just eleven years,
a life we need to keep in view.
    Did soldiers need of him have fears?

Close by a Gazan fence he stood;
    he wore no bombs, he had no gun.
Yet soldiers dared to spill his blood,
    and now he'll never play or run.

Must one now plead for children's rights
    within so-called democracy?
More violence simply invites
    more government hypocrisy.

Another Palestinian dead!
    Who'll mourn him in a synagogue?
Another child shot in the head!
    Death's cruel, shameful monologue!

In mosques, in churches mourn this child,
    in synagogues mourn him as well,
Young Yaser pleads, "Be reconciled!
    Make peace out of this living hell."

---

1. Yaser Abu al-Naja became the 16th Palestinian child to be killed by Is-raeli forces in the Gaza Strip since March 30. On Friday afternoon, June 29, 2018, as Israeli soldiers from the other side of the fence were firing tear gas, rubber bullets, and live ammunition, Yaser Abu al-Naja and a few friends took cover behind a waste container adjacent to the fence. Yaser was shot in the head and died immediately.

Let common prayers for him be said,
    let Yaser not have died in vain!
Yes, let his name with peace be wed!
        Perhaps we then can stand the pain.

14. No One Like You

There'll never be another you,
    a thought to ponder now.
Yes, even a child you never knew—
    a thought some scarce allow.

A child from Gaza or from Qom,
    no one will be like him.
Even when she's taken from her home
    and future hope seems dim.

This boy and girl are both unique;
    no one with them compares.
Dare you on them such havoc wreak
    by showing no one cares?

They sit in prison all alone,
    their families torn apart,
while you sit by and this condone:
    the Pontius Pilate art!

Among these children there might be
    a scientist or judge.
Yet who is going to set them free?
    Do you their lives begrudge?

Wake up, you thoughtless criminals,
    lest future brilliant minds
you turn into subliminals,
    not into masterminds.

Each child deserves the right to grow,
    its mind and talents too.
It's only then we all can know
    that you *alone* are you!

15. Evil Cares Not

The children played, stopped, turned around,
    the earth a bomb blast ripped;
They all lay prone upon the ground
    and of their garments stripped.

There were just six of them that day,
    four young girls, young boys two,
who'd gone outside a while to play,
    an hour before curfew.

Naked and still there dead they lay,
    but one struggled to move,
for only one survived that day,
    as hideous fate did prove.

The hideous fate these children proved
    is: evil cares not who
from life, it will or has removed;
    it cares not that you're you.

War mongers have a single goal:
    to conquer and oppress.
Five children's lives that day they stole,
    each parent's warm caress.

All those who foster hate and fear
    in children, take their lives,
deserve strongest rebuke, severe;
    no good from them survives.

It matters not culture or creed,
    a Christian, Moslem, Jew,
Each child from hatred must be freed
    to live, to self be true.

16. PTSD[1] and Palestinian Children

The Palestinian children struck
    with terrible PTSD,
were wakened by a soldiers' truck
    that stopped by their big olive tree.

The tree stood by their own front door,
    the clanging truck doors opened, shut.
They heard loud footsteps more, then more,
    each child then faced a rifle butt.

One soldier holding a large gun,
    then pointed it at sister's head.
At three years she knew not to run
    or they might shoot one of us dead.

I was just eight years old that year,
    ev'n I knew how insane this was.
At three years sis caused no one fear,
    yet she was caught in hatred's jaws.

Our house was turned inside and out,
    as soldiers hoped something to find.
But we all knew without a doubt
    their goal: to wreck each person's mind.

We did not know PTSD
    we children for the years to come
would suffer, yes, unendingly,
    while Israel's leaders thought, "Ho, hum."

A crime of crimes: threaten a child,
    so it is lifelong terrified.

---

1. Post traumatic stress disorder.

Thus, Israel's nation is reviled;
its ancient prophets mortified.

17. Unforgivable Child Terror

A child turned 'round, her life was changed,
    a miracle she was not hurt.
She did not know what was arranged
    to turn her home to rubble, dirt.

There was a warning, an alarm;
    some soldiers came, spoke not a word.
It mattered not if they did harm.
    A giant blast was all she heard.

She thought her parents were nearby,
    but all she saw was clouds of smoke.
Beneath a tree she sat to cry,
    so terrified, no word she spoke.

Then through the smoke her father came
    and took her in his warm embrace.
She sobbed and tried to speak his name.
    They looked for their house, not a trace.

The house where she was born was gone.
    The terror of the giant blast
would haunt her from that moment on.
    This terror would her lifelong last!

18. A Palestinian Child in Prison

Who cares what happens to a child
    whose birthplace is in Palestine?
Should Israel's action be defiled:
    a child in prison to confine?

When Palestinian boys and girls
    in military prisons land,
where hateful cruelty unfurls,
    one loses mother's tender hand.

Perhaps they're charged with no offence.
    allowed no visitors or bail,
no legal counsel for defense.
    With each attempt the parents fail.

"He's a small boy who meant no harm,
    when skipping stones across our pond.
He's not seen soldiers at our farm
    and did not see them just beyond . . .

"beyond the water's glistening edge,
    amid the sunbeam's shimmering light.
No matter what you may allege
    he was not trying to start a fight."

19. A Family Somewhere in Gaza, Yemen, Iraq

He was rugged,
fatigued, and worn.
He grimaced slightly;
no one knew why.
There was no time
for nourishment,
no time for health.
His hungry children
broke his heart.
Hannah, his wife,
lay slowly dying.
The fear of dysentery
haunted the household.
The eldest daughter
took the few cents
her father earned
to buy milk
for the week.
A deadly silence
filled the room,
as if sound
had never existed.
A chill ran through
their bodies
from the dank,
earthen floor.
The mother spoke
tenderly to each child.
They gathered round
kissing her cheeks.
The milk arrived;
the children drank.
The father held
his wife's hand

as she took
her last breath.
The day ended.

Section 3

Faith

20. Psalm 10

In times of trouble do you hide
like those who poor cannot abide?
Or are you caught in your own schemes
that take your greed to high extremes?
And should prosperity you find,
will sharing it be on your mind?
Would you dare say, "I'll not be moved"?
Must desperate needs to you be proved?
The selfish, poor folk will ignore,
for charity they find a chore.
If you do your part for the poor,
you'll strengthen hearts, that is quite sure.
Do justice for all those in need,
so is the earth of terror freed.

21. A Holy Land Disgrace

In Israel disaster reigns:
    it takes Palestinian land.
As Israel its history stains,
    dare it be called the Holy Land?

Its ads for tourists make this claim
    but hopes no one will dare to see
that ethnic cleansing is an aim
    of Israel's land-grab policy.

Disgrace this is for Holy Land
    where three great religions were born,
and should for justice take a stand,
    yet Palestinians are forlorn.

Will Israel justice defy;
    it's prophet's justice cry[1] ignore?
If so, God's will it does deny:
    "Love, justice for all!" will deplore.

---

1. Amos 5:24, "Let justice roll down like rivers and righteousness like an ever-flowing stream."

22. Israel's New God[2]

These are your gods, O Israel,
    who brought you up out of Egypt.
And now you act like Jezebel:
    cast landowners into a crypt.

Your golden calf is now the land;
    you worship it as your own god:
"We're given it by God's own hand
    and every meter of the sod."

With this audacious claim, you make
    of God an unjust, wicked thief:
Your God supports you when you take
    a farmer's land without relief?

If God relented in the past
    'gainst Israel of a burning wrath,
how long will God's relenting last
    while Israel takes this evil path.

2. Exodus 32:7–10: The Lord said to Moses, "Go down at once! Your people, whom you brought up out of the land of Egypt, have acted perversely; they have been quick to turn aside from the way I commanded them; they have cast for themselves an image of a [golden] calf, and have worshiped it and sacrificed to it, and said, 'These are your gods, O Israel, who brought you up out of the land of Egypt!'" The Lord said to Moses, "I have seen this people, how stiff-necked they are. Now let me alone, so that my wrath may burn against them and I may consume them; and of you I will make a great nation."

23. Al Khalil / Hebron

What has become of Al Khalil,
    the city known of Abraham?
Now marred by tensions one can feel,
    which make of history a sham.

Three faiths this city venerate,
    where saints of theirs in peace now rest.
Today the city teems with hate,
    by Jewish settlers it's distressed.

They settle high above the street,
    where Palestinians live below.
Some throw their garbage at their feet.
    Must humans really stoop so low?

How can the Christians, Muslims, Jews
    honor the saints of Al Khalil?
Perhaps all three should share the news:
    "We'll show the world our faiths are real."

"We'll trust our saints died not in vain.
    We'll trust our common heritage.
Like Abraham, faith we'll not feign:
    We'll look to God in every age."

24. Love Whom You Choose?

Love others as you love yourself,
a premise some put on the shelf.
For Jews and Christians, it's a rule;
If they ignore, they play the fool.
For faith, you may not pick and choose
the scriptures you prefer, or lose.
You lose the right your faith to claim;
and worst, you give it a bad name.
When Jesus spoke for neighbor love,
he meant no law can be above,
above the love for humankind,
no matter what is on your mind.
So Jews must love those not like them;
the Palestinians not condemn.
And Christians too must love the Jews
and Muslims, not just whom they choose.
These faiths together all could show:
"Love one another," that they know.

25. Love Your Neighbor

A family we are of Jews,
    for centuries we have lived here.
Our Arab friends did not refuse
    to help us farm each row and tier
of land that bordered on their farm.
    We shared our vegetables and grain.
Our different faiths caused no alarm,
    our friendship we need not explain.

Boys Ahmed, Samuel played each day,
    as children always want to do.
These childhood neighbors found a way
    to speak both languages they knew.
As bosom pals, they grew to men
    together built a cabinet shop
and did not dream of a day when
    their lives as neighbors soon could stop.

A war and years of pain then came
    with Ahmed's family house destroyed.
Their land was taken, and with shame,
    it seemed a friendship might be void.
Yet, both men knew no state or law
    could take away humanity
received at birth without a flaw,
    or that would be insanity.

When Ahmed sought land to reclaim,
  he was arrested, sent to jail.
But Samuel knew it was a frame
  and went at once to post his bail.
Though Samuel knew he'd risk a lot,
  a Palestinian to befriend,
he thought, I'll do what I was taught:
  I'll love my neighbor to the end.

26. Who Knows God's Will?

In Palestine there lived a man,
 a Palestinian Christian.
His friends who lived by the Quran,
 most understood his position.
But not the occupying Jews,
 who took his father's land and home,
and said, "We'll take land as we choose."
 like rulers of vast, ancient Rome:

His parents taught him love always
 those who despitefully use you.
Ev'n if they set your home ablaze,
 do not let hatred change your view.
The Christian could not understand,
 for Hebrew Scriptures clearly say:
"Your neighbor, love," is the command,[1]
 "as you yourself love" day by day!

Today the so-called "Jewish" state
 abandons its own heritage,
and chooses "greed" life to dictate.
 With violence now it sets the stage
to claim what rightfully belongs
 to others who for ages past
were dwellers there! What are their wrongs?
 They are not Jews! Their die is cast!

Throughout the world elsewhere today
 this "ethnic cleansing" would be named.
But Zionist Jews are bold to say:
 "It's God's will and we're not ashamed!"

---

1. Leviticus 19:18, "You shall not take vengeance or bear a grudge against any of your people, but you shall love your neighbor as yourself: I am the Lord."

And evangelical Christians too
    now share this radical wrong view:
"The state of Israel's a break through,
    for we God's will for Israel knew."

Does God will hatred and vile greed?
    What Holy Scriptures tell this tale?
Has God no sense of human need,
    and makes of greed a Holy Grail?
Do you think God wills bias, hate,
    where love of neighbor suffers long?
Would God then will a Jewish state
    where lack of justice causes wrong?[1]

1. Leviticus 19:15, "You shall not render an unjust judgment; you shall not be partial to the poor or defer to the great: with justice you shall judge your neighbor."

27. The Breach

O, "Pray for Jerusalem's peace!"[2]
    for centuries, one said.
Yet centuries brought its decrease,
    as violence has spread.

In Zion city there's no peace,
    and on that holy hill
all law enforcement's by police,
    for peace is a lost skill.

While God's insulted Spirit cries
    in mosque, church, synagogue,
the wisdom of the ages dies;
    it's lost in hatred's fog.

The Bible and the Quran teach:
    Love, mercy, peace for all.
God's Spirit weeps when there's a breach
    behind each cap, prayer shawl.

No matter if you cleanse your hands,
    formalities fulfill,
think not your prayers God understands,
    when you reject God's will.

God's will is this: show love to all,
    both sacred books aver.
All acts of hatred God appall!
    and God's own will deter!

---

2. Psalm 122:6, "Pray for the peace of Jerusalem."

Section 4

Injustice

28. A Woman in White — Rouzan al-Najjar[1]

(Her name: Rouzan al-Najjar, a volunteer medic
dressed in a white uniform)

A medic, she had come that day,
    if someone help should need,
as demonstrators have their say,
    and "Justice! Justice!" plead.

While Palestinians come in peace,
    (with soldiers standing by),
and chant: "Let justice never cease,"
    Rouzan in white would die.

Even if Israeli soldiers fired,
    some thought, into the air
to scatter those of whom they'd tired,
    Rouzan in white was there,

was there right where a bullet fell
    and struck her in the heart.
I shudder of her fate to tell,
    for peace it tears apart.

1. According to a report in the *New York Times* an Israeli sniper fired into a crowd where medics with white coasts were standing. When portions of videos and photographs from hundreds of people in attendance were used to reconstruct the event in which one of the medics, Rouzan al-Najjar, was killed, it was clear that she posed no threat to anyone. She was there to assist anyone who might need help. Israel claimed that her death was unintentional. No one has ever been charged or punished for her death.

See www.nytimes.com/2018/12/30/world/middleeast/gaza-medic-israel-shooting.html

29. Who Is an Anti-Semite?

1. Who is an anti-Semite?
    Someone hostile toward Jews,
  criticizes out of spite,
    and others would abuse.

2. Today there's great confusion,
    for Israel of late
  has come to the conclusion
    that it's a Jewish state.

3. But what of Palestinians
    who've lived for ages there?
  There are widespread opinions
    that Israel does not care.

4. How strange is such a viewpoint;
    Jews suffered centuries long.
  Why peace now with hate anoint?
    Right must replace the wrong.

5. How can a state be Jewish?
    Religious it is not.
  But it is very shrewish,
    for "Haves," "Have nots" they've got.

6. "Have nots" are Palestinians,
    the "enemies" of state
  some of them are citizens,
    albeit second rate.

7. What would the Hebrew prophets,
    who pled for justice streams,
  say of Israeli profits
    gained by deceptive schemes?

8. If one then should criticize
    the so-called Jewish state,
  is this anti-Semite's guise
    or an honest debate?

9. Critique of Israel the state
    is every person's right.
  Critique is healthy, not hate;
    it's not anti-Semite!

10. Can return the days of old
    when Palestinian, Jew,
  side by side tilled land and told
    their stories old and new?

30. Inhumane Governing

There is no hope and no relief
    when governments are inhumane.
Their citizens face the belief:
    that life's no more than constant pain.

They confiscate the land of those
    who're powerless this to resist.
Should one the government oppose,
    soon it will raise an angry fist.

Its angry fist in justice's guise,
    pretends the right of noble cause,
but cannot hide from all who're wise,
    such justice breaches humane laws.

There's no such thing as "right divine,"
    no people, nation this may claim.
For justice, words like "yours" and "mine"
    result so oft in endless blame.

31. Khan al-Ahmar Doomed[1]

"We must destroy your house today,"
    Israeli COGAT[2] said.
"And call us if you dare to say,
    'This, this I truly dread.'"

"Our staff is managing the phones;
    "they'll help you with this task.
"Just phone them quickly or the drones
    "leave you nothing to ask.

"To Bedouins of Khan al-Ahmar:
    "We're ready to assist.
"We'll make your lives better by far,
    "so please do not resist.

"Feel free to give us now a call,
    "the number is toll free,
"We'll help you tear down every wall.
    "Thank you, that you agree!

"You say, we occupy your land,
    "but how can this then be?
"We won the war and we have planned
    "to share the victory.

1. On September 23rd, 2018, Israeli authorities ordered the residents of Khan al-Ahmar Bedouin community to demolish their houses and school by Monday, October 1st. To make matters worse, Israeli authorities included a phone number in the demolition order, which was provided in case the residents need assistance in demolishing their own homes.

2. COGAT = Coordinator of Government Activities in the Territories

"This is God's plan for faithful Jews,
    "and we regret the fact
"that this brings Bedouins sad news,
    "but we just have to act.

"Our settlements change Bedouin shacks
    "to homes of sound cement,
"though olives trees we have to axe,
    "please, progress don't lament!"

32. A Bourgeois Thought

How can one evil justify,
    to others be unfair?
Make others hunger and to die
    and offer no one care?

In Israel, Yemen, Palestine,
    Somalia, US too,
most poor folk have no chance to dine
    with likes of me and you.

One moment, do you dare suggest
    that I such evil will?
Most surely you intend a jest!
    Goodwill my interests fill.

But goodwill oft spells apathy,
    perhaps a state of mind.
Even if you're filled with sympathy,
    do you act thus in kind?

I know I should remember well,
    for it indeed is so:
one's lost intent the soul will sell,
    Mephisto's in the know.

33. The 1948-Nakba Fraud[1]

"No one made Palestinians flee;
they left their homes quite willingly.
They left their houses and their lands,
they left them in Israeli hands."
Those UN photographs, a fraud,
the *Nakba* is an idea flawed.
Even so, the photos tell the tale
of how the exit was wholesale.
The Palestinian exit, yes,
for which there could be no redress.
The *Nakba*, Israel now derides,
that's why all documents it hides.
The documents that tell the truth
make Israel a bumbling sleuth:
Destroy all papers and all files
so, there can never be just trials.
No Palestinians have the right
to reclaim land, for they took flight.
The *Nakba* never did take place.
Leave not of it a single trace!

---

1. The exodus of Palestinians in 1948, is commonly known as the *Nakba* (Arabic: النكبة, al-Nakbah, which means "disaster," "catastrophe," or "cataclysm"). At that time more than 700,000 Palestinian Arabs, about half of the Palestinian Arab prewar population, fled or were forced from their homes and land, during the 1948 Palestine war. Between 400 and 600 Palestinian villages were attacked and/or destroyed during the war. At the following website one finds the story of the attempt to destroy evidence related to these events: https://israelpalestinenews.org/how-israel-systematically-hides-evidence-of-1948-expulsion-of-arabs/.

34. A Reason Why?

Is there no recourse, but despair,
when violence is in the air?
When fathers, mothers, children die,
and death life's meaning would decry.
When bombs and bullets tear apart
life's chances long before they start.
Will burning flesh, its odor, reign
across a hillside's vast terrain?
Who's left to dig the needed graves?
Is all that's left a life of slaves?
For those who make this life a hell,
can destiny reverse the spell?
Resist one must the spell they cast;
resist, resist, it cannot last!
Resist one must or there's no hope!
Resist one must or one can't cope!
It's better to resist and die
than live without a reason why!

35. Another Year

One starts again another year,
but constant is the fear on fear.
The hungry starve and children die,
and desperate parents ask, "Why? Why?"
There still are warlords in Sudan,
and Souleimani of Iran
the US killed with lethal speed
to satisfy an ego need:
to boast, "This makes the US great!"—
yet soldiers leaves to perilous fate.
While politicians fold their hands,
the wars rage on in Mid-East lands.
As Yemen wreaks of raging war;
its children cry and ask, "What for?"
While Israel swallows Palestine,
its generals toast success with wine.
Is there no hope throughout the earth
that peace at last can have new birth?

36. One Israeli's View

So many Gazans died today.
Attackers, what have you to say?
The children, innocent, you've killed!
Was this indeed what you had willed?
"We'll tell you now of our intent:
"To cleanse this land, we have been sent.
"No innocents in Gaza live,
"So, death to them, we freely give!
"The Gazans have no right to life!
"They make for Israel only strife!
"God's creatures surely they are not!
"With death, they thus have cast their lot."

37. Oppression

Oppression is the worst of life.
No, no grim gesture, grimmest strife!
Dictators with a laugh, or frown,
keep crushing people down and down.

Stripped of possessions, home, and land
oppressors take all that's at hand,
that could let some at least survive,
but best, they think, let no one thrive.

How many lands does this describe—
this endless, blistering diatribe?
Israel, Syria, Palestine,
Yemen and Lebanon combine,

combine to show the world the loss
of true humanity and dross,
the dross which power does not see
for its self-focus sets it free,

free for egregrious power abuse
to treat its victims like refuse.
This is the creed that hatred knows;
this is the creed the world it shows.

Oppression cannot rule for aye;
most surely there's another way:
The way of human love and peace
alone can make oppression cease.

38. Possession

Possession does the world consume,
a right presumptuous some assume:
they take, possess all that they want;
their power over weak folk flaunt.

Sometimes they're subtle in their art,
yet lives of others tear apart.
At times, they act like righteous ones,
but take possession with their guns.

They think with money they can buy
all that they want. Do not ask why!
Example, by no means the least:
Trump's peace plan for the Middle East.

For Palestinians lands possessed,
the Trump solution is the best:
All that the Palestinians need
is money with which they'll be freed.

So Israel simply takes their land,
and Palestine, the name, is banned.
Then US, Israel save the day
and build new parks where children play.

But on that land once farmer's seed
filled Palestinians' many a need.
Possession, money, evil are,
when used the human needs to bar.

Possession is a worthy goal
when its design is for the whole,
is for the whole of humankind,
a plan with loving care designed.

39. War Games

The violence in Gaza grows
as anyone who's sane well knows.
Abduction, murder, fill the air
as no one stops the violent flair.
One reads the numbers like baseball:
the scores are ones that us appall!—
Teenagers, three Israelis, yes
abducted, murdered with redress:
a young Palestinian teen
was burned and killed, a death obscene!
The score is thus then three to one,
but who cares now what has been done?
Hamas fires rockets in the air,
Israelis drop bombs without care.
Who's keeping score of rockets, bombs,
while no one brings poor people alms?

40. Why Others Blame and Maim?

A synagogue, a mosque, a church
    are daily scenes of prayer;
but some would such a place besmirch
    and create many a scare.

A scare with weapons, knives, and guns,
    to kill those who're at prayer
no one is safe, even little ones.
    It matters not who's there.

Misguided rage vented on those,
    who live by different views,
gives no one right them to oppose:
    Christians, Moslems, or Jews.

Rage creates problems and divides;
    helps no one else to see
another point of view; it hides
    the yearn for victory.

Till humans dissipate their rage,
    their violence and hate,
they're prisoners in their own cage
    of misery's mandate.

Each one of us indeed was born,
    conceived by nature's plan.
The birth of no one need we mourn,
    nor rights of humans ban.

At birth we were so much alike;
    this truth do not forget!
Remember to be more childlike—
    without the need of threat!

We all are born, we all will die,
    in birth and death the same.
If so alike, then question why
    we others blame and maim.

41. Who Cares?

Who cares about the Middle East?
    In Israel, the decades pass—
no step toward peace, no, not the least!
    And Palestinians are second class.

A refugee in one's own land?
    In one's own land? How can this be?
One's house is taken by demand,
    demand of government decree.

A stranger in one's own homeland,
    a stranger stripped of dignity.
Is no one left who'll take a stand
    to wipe out hate and bigotry?

The Mid-East crisis soars and soars
    as countries flood with refugees.
They're poor and cannot shop in stores;
    their hunger daily each child sees.

Compassion is completely lost
    among most nations of the earth.
And they are doomed to pay the cost
    when truth and justice have no worth.

42. What Happened to the Promised Land?

What happened to the promised land,
    and to whom did the promise come?
What of the water and the sand
    where many tribes had made their home?
A rabbi said abundant life,
    a gift divine, was made to all,
but promised land meant only strife
    where victors would o'ercome the small.

Both water, land, life's precious source
    of sustenance for every tribe,
caused war and taking both by force,
    which sacred pages well describe.
The Canaanites, the Israelites—
    which one do you think God preferred?
After the dreadful, warring fights,
    the victors claim it is absurd—

absurd to ask, when those who've won,
    know God is always on their side.
What evil on this earth is done
    when those who win, others deride!
They take from war the victor's spoils,
    land, water with which to survive.
And with resistance hate recoils;
    sometimes no one is left alive.

What is the promised land today?
  a land with large *moshavs*[1] in bloom,
where Palestinian farms decay
  and settlers leave them no more room.
Can this the land of promise be,
  a land by hate and ill will ruled?
God's promise is not cruelty:
  by lust and greed God is not fooled!

So, love your neighbor, friend, and foe,
  creation's glorious landscape art,
each stream, each mountain, sunset glow,
  our thoughts, our intellect, each part
of life that wills to drive us on,
  each human being from its start
in life from morning, night, and dawn
  till love fills every human heart.

---

1. *Moshav* (plural, *Moshavim*) is a cooperative association of Israeli smallholders.

Section 5

Peace

43. Being Human

In ancient Palestine the wars
    were not just mere hearsay.
Like angry, wrestling dinosaurs,
    one tribe would others slay.

Disputes of power, water, land,
    malicious tyrants made.
War, slavery, and murder planned;
    the poor they gave no aid.

The Philistines and Canaanites
    both ravaged land and folk.
They conquered, took away their rights,
    religion made a joke.

What of the Hittites, Moabites
    and hosts of other tribes.
Josephus oft their crimes recites,
    injustices describes.

Is Palestine better today
    where war, injustice reign?
Where occupation has its way,
    and peace is no one's gain!

In Palestine can Arab, Jew
    be friends and live in peace?
Their history seems to teach that few
    exchange love for caprice.

Is Palestine better today
    where Arabs, Jews still die?
Where being human day by day
    struggles against a lie:

the lie that someone has the right
    to take another's land,
dehumanizes this dire plight,
    for civil rights are banned.

In being human there's a chance
    to live in peace not strife,
to have in every circumstance
    respect for each one's life.

44. Peace, Peace, but there's No Peace[1]

"Peace, peace, they cry, but there's no peace."
    This message is not new.
Since time began, wars do not cease,
    with warring bands in queue,
in queue to strike the next death blow,
    one knows not where or when.
But human greed will make it so:
    the world's a lion's den,

a lion's den of evil greed
    that tears all flesh apart,
with disregard for human need,
    thrives on a hardened heart.
The hardened heart violence condones
    and human beings kills
with newest weapons, bombing drones,
    and children learn these skills.

Can nothing stop this evil strain?
    Only a common will
that greed and violence restrain,
    with peace the world will fill.
Lay down all arms, make peace the goal,
    think of each child you see.
Heal broken lives and make them whole.
    Let your will peace decree.

---

1. "They have dressed the wound of my people with very little care, saying, 'Peace, peace,' when there is no peace at all. They dress the wound of my people as though it were not serious. 'Peace, peace,' they say, when there is no peace. They offer superficial treatments for my people's mortal wound" (Jeremiah 6:14).

45. Peace of Jerusalem

For peace pray for Jerusalem.[2]
    May those who love you be secure.
A constant sounding diadem
    of peace be your allure.

Who are Jerusalem's lovers,
    whose heritage they share,
whose choir of saints o'er her hovers,
    the source of constant prayer?

Since Christians, Muslims, and the Jews
    Jerusalem all love,
in our day it should not be news—
    All hatred she's above.

Above revenge and hate and fear
    we sense within her gates
a holy city atmosphere,
    and yet for peace she waits.

2. Psalm 122:6
Pray for the peace of Jerusalem,
may they be secure who love you.

46. Progress and Peace

If you pursue progress and peace,
    you'll find they have no end.
The quest for both can never cease;
    they on pursuit depend.

No victory nor a defeat
    fulfills all of their goals.
Never are progress, peace complete;
    they cost the trial of souls.

Their errors and successes few,
    or manifold they be,
require them further to pursue
    with full capacity.

47. "First Do No Harm"

Can it be that "first do no harm"
    becomes what is done last?
And one is stunned, shocked with alarm—
    the chance one had, is past.

"First do no harm," but take the land
    to which you have no right?
With thievery by your own hand,
    put justice out of sight?

This makes "first do no harm" a sham,
    a travesty, a fraud,
and turns all justice to a scam,
    when thieves act like they're god.

What if in Israel, Palestine,
    "First do no harm" became
the slogan of each party line?
    No one would others maim.

Can human beings really make
    to "do no harm" the key
to acting for each other's sake?
    If not, no one is free.

Enslave is oft what humans do!
    But what if they could see:
"first do no harm" was done to you
    and also done to me?

48. A Prevent-Peace Tactic

The tactic to prevent a peace
    in Israel, Palestine
gives settlers time more land to fleece;
    to take it, call it "mine."

Seek peace! No, that's the wrong desire;
    the settlers want delay.
They want more time land to acquire.
    This is the easy way.

Act out the part, "It's peace we want."
    Put obstacles in place
to camouflage clever détente,
    and old land claims erase.

Right now a "Jewish State" supports
    the settlers' unjust claims,
and there's no recourse in the courts
    'gainst ethnic cleansing aims.

49. Children of Abraham

Still in the land of Palestine
    three great religions plead for peace.
And yet for hope there is no sign,
    for hate and violence do not cease.

The talk of many is a sham,
    sincerity is a lost art.
How sad children of Abraham
    their lives and others tear apart.

Children of Abraham, beware:
    his children should the nations bless,
not foster gross, non-stop warfare.
    Alas, they must now peace confess!

50. One State

For years in Palestine the cry
    has been "two states we need,"
but decades pass and thousands die,
    while two states yield to greed.

Today there's an apartheid state
    which clearly favors Jews,
and Palestinians face the fate:
    they're destined all to lose,

unless one state, justice for all,
    can one day come to be,
where no one's trapped behind a wall,
    and all are truly free.

One person and one vote for all
    regardless of one's race.
Jews, Muslims, Christians overhaul
    laws humans that disgrace.

One state, one state instead of two
    alone is just and right.
One state for justice, a breakthrough.
    It's worthy of a fight.

Bibliography

Carter, Jimmy. *Palestine: Peace Not Apartheid.* Reprint Edition. New York: Simon and Schuster, 2007.

Finkelstein, Norman. *The Holocaust Industry: Reflections on the Exploitation of Jewish Suffering.* New York: Verso, 2000.

Hass, Amira. *Drinking the Sea at Gaza: Days and Nights in a Land Under Siege.* New York: Henry Holt, 1999.

Khalidi, Rashid. *The Hundred Years' War on Palestine: A History of Settler Colonization and Resistence 1917–2017.* New York: Metopolitan, 2020.

Kimbrough, S T, Jr. *Why Should a Child Be Born? Poems for Peace and Justice in the Middle East.* Eugene, OR: Resource, 2018.

Masalha, Nur. *Imperial Israel and the Palestinians: the Politics of Expansion.* New York: Pluto, 2000.

Morris, Benny. *Righteous Victims: A History of the Zionist-Arab Conflict, 1881–1999.* New York: Knopf, 1999.

Pappe, Ilan, ed. *Israel/Palestine Question: Rewriting Histories.* New York: Routledge, 1999.

Raheb, Mitri. *Faith in the Face of Empire: the Bible through Palestinian Eyes.* Maryknoll, NY: Orbis, 2014.

———. *Bethlehem Besieged. Stories of Hope in Times of Trouble.* Minneapolis: Augsburg Fortress, 2004.

Said, Edward. *The End of the Peace Process: Oslo and After.* New York: Parthenon, 2000.

www.ingramcontent.com/pod-product-compliance
Lightning Source LLC
LaVergne TN
LVHW021614080426
835510LV00019B/2558